Pathfinder 16

A CILT series for language teachers

Not bothered?

Motivating reluctant language learners in Key Stage 4

Jenifer Alison

C*i*LT

Other titles in the PATHFINDER series:

Acknowledgements

The pupils I 'borrowed'; their teachers who lent them to me and who gave me so much support and advice. Steven Fawkes, Advisory Teacher for Durham; James Burch, Principal Lecturer for Modern Languages, and Michelle Gibbins, Head of Modern Languages Department, Upholland High School; the teachers who during workshops and conferences all over Britain so readily shared their experiences and ideas. The Languages Development Centre, S. Martin's College for allowing me to reproduce here my materials for the *Modern Language Skills for Work* scheme.

First published 1993
Copyright © 1993 Centre for Information on Language Teaching and Research
ISBN 1 874016 06 2

Cover by Logos Design & Advertising
Printed in Great Britain by Oakdale Printing Co. Ltd.

Published by Centre for Information on Language Teaching and Research, 20 Bedfordbury, London WC2N 4LB

Contents

Foreword

Throughout this book references are made to a project I undertook in 1990-91 which involved teaching the class of low attaining pupils in year 10 at an urban mixed 11-18 comprehensive school, which operated a languages-for-all policy from 11-16.

I was involved with this class for a year and continued to follow their progress throughout their year 11. During years 10 and 11 they attempted two modules of the *Preliminary Certificate in Modern Language Skills for Work* scheme*, and then they went on to attempt GCSE. They all achieved a grade. My congratulations to them!

References to what happened during that time have been used to illustrate points made throughout the book. They appear in large quotation marks every time. The comments which appear in this way are often related to the activities outlined in Chapter 6.

* (Information about this scheme can be obtained from the Languages Development Centre, S. Martin's College, Lancaster LA1 3JD. Tel: 0524 32423.)

Further reading

It is difficult to find material specifically relating to this age group but the following titles contain a good deal of relevant advice.

Modern languages and children with special educational needs in ordinary schools, Alan Armstrong. *A Pre-vocational approach to GCSE*. Lancs LEA documents produced in association with the Languages Development Centre, S. Martin's College.

Documentation from the CILT Languages and Special Needs Project (set up January 1991).

'Teaching modern languages to pupils with special needs? With pleasure!' Michele Dean, University of Bath. *ALL Journal* No. 6.

Foreign languages in tourism: a programme for active learning for 14-16 year olds. North Yorkshire Language Centre.

Introduction

From September 1995 it will be statutory under the National Curriculum for every pupil in Key Stage 4 to learn a foreign language.

Because most schools offer a foreign language to all pupils in years 7-9, many of us are used to teaching a wide ability range in the option groups in years 10 and 11. Whatever their level of attainment, these pupils have chosen (in most cases) to continue learning a second language, so we would assume that they are reasonably well motivated.

The statutory entitlement to the study of a foreign language for **all** pupils in years 10 and 11 will mean that an increased number of teachers will find pupils in their classes **who have not chosen** to be there.

Some of them will have been reasonably, or even very successful up until the end of year 9, and they - and their teachers - will be pleased that the National Curriculum entitles them to continue with the study of a foreign language.

Others, for various reasons, will have experienced failure and frustration. Many of them may be dismayed that they have to continue this situation for another two years, convinced that they 'can't do it!'

This latter group is catered for in two main ways in the considerable number of schools which already operate a languages-for-all policy in years 10-11. In some schools they are dispersed into mixed ability groups, whereas in others they are setted according to attainment and are concentrated in the 'bottom' set(s).

Here we are concerned with these lower sets, which contain a mixture of the willing (those who would have opted anyway under the old system) and the unwilling (those who wouldn't have chosen). It's the latter, the low attaining and **reluctant** learners, who can have such a negative influence on the atmosphere in the classroom.

What are these classes like?

They can vary in attitude and outlook. In some classes, for instance, the pupils are happy just to sit and write as long as we don't disturb them too much by asking them to perform tasks which involve using the foreign language. In other classes, however, the pupils are capable of leaving their teacher feeling totally at a loss, depressed and inadequate at the end of the lesson. These are the pupils who take up what seems a disproportionate amount of our thinking and preparation time and who are in our minds in the early hours of the morning as we puzzle out what makes them tick and what we can try next.

I hope to be able to present some ways of approaching this problem.

1.   What are these pupils like?

Task

If you have a difficult year 10 group at the moment, think about those pupils for a second or two and jot down all the words that you feel would describe them.

If your school doesn't yet operate a languages-for-all policy in years 10 and 11, then list the words which you think will describe the kind of pupils you will be teaching.

Now look below. The characteristics you see listed come from various brainstorming sessions with practising teachers during workshop days. Compare this list with yours.

Bored ★ Crude	Can't concentrate ★ Lazy
Tired ★ Careless	Absent ★ Fidgety
Won't learn ★ Impulsive	Rude ★ Moody
Forget ★ Untidy	Noisy ★ Late
Inattentive ★ Touchy	Emotionally disturbed ★ Inaccurate
Loud ★ Don't do homework	A difference between the ★ Different from
Jealous ★ Resentful	morning and the afternoon one day to the next
Aggressive ★ Just want to write	

The project involved teaching these year 10 pupils first lesson on Monday and Tuesday mornings for an hour. There was a noticeable difference in their performance and attitude between the Monday and the Tuesday. On occasions on a Monday morning they would arrive in a difficult mood. Who knows what they had had to contend with over the weekend? Tuesday's lessons were often more productive.

When are you at your best, Paul?
About Tuesday... (Evaluation session)

What makes these classes difficult to teach?

Some in the class are keen to progress. However, they are often swamped by the others who seem to take it in turns to disrupt proceedings. It's difficult to predict how these individuals will react from one lesson to the next. They tend to drift into the lessons, often late, sometimes half asleep, sometimes already in an evil mood! It's a major struggle to separate them from their anoraks!

Establish relationships of mutual trust and respect

How can we create this feeling of trust and respect with these pupils?

- Find moments to be able to talk with individuals on a personal level.

What do we talk about?

Their interests, their hopes for the future, their progress so far, their problems. Talk about our own interests and our lives as far as we feel is appropriate. In this way we gradually become a real person to them and, as they begin to trust us as an adult friend, they will be more prepared to speak about themselves. Also, in the classroom, they will begin to react to us in a more respectful way. With some pupils this can be a very long process, full of ups and downs, and can demand a great deal of tact.

When can we find time to do this?

This is very difficult during the lesson. Perhaps take ten minutes at the end now and then to chat to the class informally in their mother tongue. If you do this at the end you have more hope of conducting the main part of the lesson in the target language.

Visits or major projects which involve your working together outside lesson time offer an excellent opportunity to narrow the gap between you and them.

The exchange of a few friendly words as you encounter them on the stairs, in the corridor - or in Tesco's, may help towards the creation of the good working relationship you are aiming for.

- Seize every opportunity to let an individual pupil know that we have thought about him/her especially, and that individual effort is recognised.

Once you get to know each pupil you can bring in material that you know is of interest to a particular individual and use that as a stimulus for language work. When marking work, it shows our interest in them if we use their names in our comments. For example, *Très bien, Paul, tu fais des progrès!*

- Set clear, manageable standards.

We need to insist that written work is properly set out and completed, then acknowledge this as soon as possible with positive comment. Marks are a motivator because the individual has tangible evidence that his/her efforts have been recognised.

> When I set up their first piece of written work I indicated they would receive a mark out of 15. That was, 10 for content plus 5 for presentation. I marked the work that evening and also added an asterisk for exceptionally well presented work. When I gave the books back the next day, the first thing they did was to compare efforts and those who had a 'star' were pleased to broadcast the fact. Even at their age! I kept to this procedure!

It's a good idea for them to have their own progress sheet with their marks recorded.

● Keep on the alert for any positive contribution

This means constantly listening and watching, not only for misdemeanours, but also even the slightest manifestation of a positive contribution. This can go unnoticed in the general bustle of the lesson or in our concern to 'get through the work' and could result in a 'Why bother' attitude of the contributor. Turn it to the good **somehow**, even if you have a struggle to see the relevance or if a mistake has been made.

We can even call their bluff. If they make silly 'throw away' suggestions, we can prevail upon them to carry them out!

> When discussing what kind of items we could put in a tourist package for French people for the local tourist office, two group members suggested a pub crawl. They were, I suppose, letting us know they knew about the things that mattered. However, they were taken up on their suggestion and asked to write out an itinerary on foot including four pubs. They found a map of the area and set to writing out the directions from one pub to another. Problems arose when they couldn't agree where they all were!

Have you ever had the situation where these pupils repeat after you in exaggerated Maurice Chevalier style? This is a wonderful opportunity to praise them for their good accent and intonation and beg them to continue!

Give them the feeling of making a useful contribution

As adults, we are far more interested in proceedings if we feel we have an important part to play in them. Our pupils are far more likely to work **with** us if we can make them feel part of the lesson. We need to make an active effort to discover their positive features. We can sometimes do this by creating situations where they come forward to offer help.

The **electronically minded** person could be responsible for the operation of the video recorder and television.

> I'd recorded part of their lesson on video and wanted to play it back on the video recorder. They were keen to see themselves, so, when I helplessly fumbled with the controls, one of them came out and took charge. We were adult to adult for that moment with him in the stronger position. Operating the video recorder and television became his job every time this equipment was used.

The **bossy** character who talks incessantly is the ideal character to start off and run a group game.

> We had a set of Teach and Test cards (see Activity 11, chapter 6.) and the bossiest most talkative person was put in charge of testing the rest of a group of four. He immediately turned it into a BBC type quiz game and the group was absorbed, speaking lots of French for all of twelve minutes!

The **imaginative** person is invaluable. We need to use the pupils' imaginations rather than exhaust our own repertoire of ways to make language learning fun for the class!

> During one lesson, I was 'slow feeding' acetate cut-outs on to the overhead projector one lesson to see who would be the first to decipher the messages on them. (See Activity 8, chapter 6.) One of them offered to be the teacher and it was surprising how many different ways there were of putting a cut-out on the projector to make it a challenge for the others to read!
>
> The pupils themselves created mimes to help them to remember the sounds of the alphabet. They were proud of their inventiveness. (See Activities 4 & 5, chapter 6.)

There may be a member of the class who turns out to be particularly **thoughtful and protective** towards the weaker members. Remember him/her if someone new arrives in the class, or if someone has been away ill and needs help to catch up.

The **tidy, meticulous** person could be in charge of the wall display.

The **soap box politician** could help with the organisation - and in fact run any main project the class may decide to take on.

> When we decided to produce a pack of materials for the local tourist office, we had a board meeting to discuss what form the pack should take, what the content should be and who should be responsible for which parts. The most difficult member of the group made a 'throw away' comment about needing a chairman. We called his bluff. He became chairman and did a most efficient job of organising the others, who listened to him far more attentively than to me. It came to light that he was involved in a council for Children in Care and therefore had experience in this field.

Make sure they see a point in what they do

As adults we would not willingly do anything which was pointless unless we were enjoying it! Yet, we expect our pupils to carry out tasks because we say so.

Higher attaining pupils do what we ask of them more readily than lower attaining groups. Even if the former do not see the point of what they are doing, they are more prepared to settle down to it. If the latter group does not see the point, however, they often react by becoming very difficult to control!

Why is this?

★ Pupils in higher attaining classes tend to be more socially mature and ready to comply with our wishes.
★ Higher attaining pupils are motivated by more distant goals, such as GCSE or the career they wish to follow.
★ Lower attaining pupils often do not conform to the school system. So, unless we can capture their interest and create tasks with an immediate purpose in their eyes we have an acute discipline problem on our hands.

So, how can we get them to see the point?

For a start, we must make sure we have a clear purpose and then look at the activity from their point of view. Will it be valid in their eyes?

A valid purpose for the pupils could be:

★ taking on a challenge - e.g. how quickly can you count to 20? (See Activity 13, chapter 6.)
★ beating the teacher - e.g. can you count faster than the teacher? (See Activity 6, chapter 6.)
★ winning a game - e.g. a board game (See Activity 7, chapter 6.)
★ creating material for other classes to use or see.

Then we need to create contexts which are at their level of maturity, which are relevant to **their** experience and in which they can become **actively involved**.

> They were keen to produce the package of materials for the tourist office and suggested inviting the tourist office director to the school to discuss it with her. They also brought information in from home. Becoming involved in major projects seemed to help them to pull together more as a group.
>
> Although at first they were worried about attempting the task alone and insisted on sitting in two's, they carried out their rôle as hotel receptionists very seriously when a group of French speakers was brought into the class posing as hotel guests. They worked for three quarters of an hour taking down details of as many guests as they could on to their hotel registration forms. *'We wanted to impress them with what we could do'* they said.
>
> They enjoyed building up a repertoire of language to refer to when carrying out tasks such as the above. One such example was a lesson where we built up a list from which they could read off days and dates in French to tell people when events were to take place in the town. They found this practical and manageable.

Avoid making them feel embarrassed by their inadequacies

Many adults find it embarrassing to have to speak in front of a large group of people for fear of losing face. There is no reason why these pupils should be any different. So, we need to avoid getting them into situations where they are made to look small in front of their contemporaries.

- We need to beware of activities which demand pupils to be in the limelight unexpectedly before we are sure that they are confident with the task they have to perform.

- We need to beware of the temptation to pounce upon someone we know hasn't been listening, knowingly putting him/her into an embarrassing situation. We've proved our point but the effect has been negative.

- We need to be careful which individual we ask to repeat in front of the class a word he/she cannot pronounce. The whole situation is aggravating and can be acutely embarrassing for the victim.

- We need to set assessment tasks only when the pupils feel confident. Although, in the end, there are set dates for tests such as GCSE, meanwhile we are assessing **progress** with a view to building confidence. So, it is not productive to set them tests we fear they will fail.

- Whenever appropriate, we could allow them to collaborate on tasks. A straightforward listening comprehension, for example, can be a far more enjoyable and valuable exercise if tackled with the support of a friend.

- We need to discover the strengths of each individual, and put him/her into a position to be able to demonstrate them to the others.

Give them encouragement

That small word of encouragement from our colleagues or from the higher échelons can have such a powerful effect on our self esteem, that we want to make even more effort to show what we can do! Many of the pupils we teach in these classes have a very low opinion of themselves and will do anything to avoid any more failure. Therefore we need to be very careful in our treatment of efforts that they do make.

We need to be sensitive in the correction of errors. We sometimes can thoughtlessly dismiss a 'wrong' response with a sharp *Non!* cutting the speaker dead and moving on to someone else. We should try to accept it as a contribution... *Merci, Susan, une bonne idée, ça* or *Oui, presque, qui peut ajouter...* etc.

Deal with their aggression with understanding

The adolescents we are dealing with in these classes often come from households where aggression is the norm. Some of these pupils may be emotionally damaged by their experiences in life and show signs of disturbed, sometimes idiosyncratic behaviour. What they do can make us feel extremely angry, especially when our self esteem is threatened. Yet, as we well know, when we shout and become angry our reward is a negative and unproductive atmosphere. Although we do need to be firm to show where our limits of tolerance are, there are some traps we can try to avoid.

- We can try to avoid **really** losing our temper and try to remain calm and positive! Firmness with humour can have the desired effect and safeguard our working relationship with them.

- We need to be careful not to stereotype. That is, we expect and wait for certain pupils to misbehave. We could try giving them all a clean slate at the beginning of every lesson.

- We should avoid pouncing on what seems to be misbehaviour until we are sure what is going on. They could be working!

3.   How can we motivate them?

Choose the appropriate content

We need to find a topic that will mean something to them. Something into which they can bring something of themselves.

It's often difficult to motivate these pupils with the fact that one day they may visit the country. *I don't want to go there anyway* is a common retort.

We need to find a content, which is:

★ adult and brings them into contact with the adult world;

★ relevant to their own experience - in order to make their foreign language learning programme appropriate to situations they can visualise themselves in one day.

One possibility would be to work towards the *Preliminary Certificate in Modern Language Skills for Work*.

The project which forms the background to this book involved spending two thirds of the pupils' modern languages lessons working towards the above certificate, and the other third on GCSE-related work.

The aim of the *Preliminary Certificate in Modern Language Skills for Work* is to *provide the learner with the basic linguistic and social skills required to cater for the needs of foreign visitors to Britain in defined tourist or work situations*. The approach is modular, and for a pupil to qualify for certification at least two modules have to have been successfully attempted. They are the compulsory core module 'Initial Contacts', and one other of the nine modules. The additional module which we chose was 'Working in Tourist Information'.

Adopting this scheme opened up all kinds of opportunities.

★ The pupils were keen to demonstrate their local knowledge.
★ We could easily establish contact with the local, adult working world and work on projects which would be useful to them.
★ The pupils were keen to impress 'real adults' (as opposed to teachers!) with their skills in the foreign language.
★ The links with local places of work were an incentive for the pupils to develop their personal and social skills.

★ They realised that if they could add the *Certificate in Modern Language Skills for Work* to their Record of Achievement, this may impress employers.

What about the National Curriculum and the other Areas of Experience?

Once the National Curriculum becomes statutory for Key Stage 4 pupils in 1995, we will have to show that we will be regularly exploring all seven Areas of Experience, of which Area D, 'The World of Education, Training and Work' is one. It would be possible to take this area as the basis of the modern languages programme for two terms of year 10, and to include other Areas within it.

The last chapters of this book list some activities, many of which relate to the context of the pupils own locality. If you look at some of these you will see, how, for example, Area E, 'The World of Communication' and Area G 'The World of Imagination and Creativity' can permeate your activities.

Ensure success

What do we have to do this for anyway? can refer to any subject on the timetable. We can bend over backwards explaining the advantages of speaking a foreign language but the pupils' outlook is often more immediate than that. They like what they are good at. This has influenced options at the age of fourteen just as much as the usefulness of the subject. So, we need to change 'I can't do that, I'm *not bothered!*' into 'I'm good at that, *it's O.K.*'

We can engineer success by building up their confidence.

★ We need to set manageable, short term goals.
★ We need to find strategies to make language memorable in the practice stages. The next chapter has examples of this.
★ We need to encourage them to discover for themselves the ways in which they learn best. Many of them equate writing with work, because, I suppose, they have tangible evidence in their books that they have done something. They feel secure and are unwilling to branch out, to attempt to communicate and therefore risk failure.

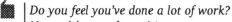

Do you feel you've done a lot of work?
Not writing, we haven't!
They always think... if you put pen to paper you've done more... but you don't learn how to say it... and talk to people and stuff like that.
(Evaluation session)

We need to offer them all sorts of different supports to 'hang' language on to. They have real problems mastering long utterances. Here, the use of rhythm is particularly effective. The teacher and the pupils find a rhythm that fits a particular phrase and it's then repeated to this same rhythm in chorus. If we can get this going, it's a good way of helping them to lose their inhibitions, because no-one can hear their individual efforts. Chanting catchy rhythms like at a football match takes their attention away from the fact that they are repeating the same words over and over again. Sometimes this can take the form of the teacher entertaining a slightly bemused and sympathetic class (*is she off her head?*) but it sinks in and some find it helpful. When we want them to use a certain phrase again we tap out the rhythm only and they produce the phrase!

 It's a good idea that rhythm effort, Miss, it helps you say it.
(Comment during a lesson)

We need to teach them to adopt strategies to **use** the language they are confident with and make it go a long way!

We need to persuade them they are not being assessed every time they open their mouths. We need to convince them that the whole point of learning a foreign language is to be able to communicate with its speakers in the real world. People achieve this to varying degrees and use all kinds of coping strategies to help communication. Part of learning a language is the development of these strategies. Here are three examples.

- Encourage them to select key words which will convey the message.

Once they realise that this is permissible instead of grappling with and trying to remember the intricacies of long sentences, they select what they really need to say.

 I don't need to say all of that, do I? I could just say, 'Quelle ville?' couldn't I?
The original question was *'Vous habitez quelle ville?'*.

- Encourage them to transfer language from one situation to another.

It can be enormously satisfying when this takes place. They might, for example, have learned to say *'I'm sorry'* in the foreign language in the context of shopping, playing the role of the shopkeeper, and then use it when they arrive late to your class! They may have learned *'Can I help you?'* in the context of working at a camp site and then use it when they offer to help you in the classroom. To do this is a skill which we need consciously to teach them.

> The assessment for the 'Initial Contacts' module involved asking and recording the foreign visitor's address.
> I was the foreign visitor and gave the number of my house as 20.
> He became very puzzled, searched the ceiling and the floor for clues, then brought his coping strategies into play.
> *Comment ça s'écrit?* he asked.
> *Deux et puis zéro,* I said, and he successfully wrote in the number twenty.

- Teach them to adopt non-verbal strategies when they fail to find the necessary language.

After all, this is what we do in real life. I once watched an Englishman and a Chinese railway worker discussing the coupling system on Chinese steam trains. This was done totally with pencil, paper, mime and facial expression!

One of the advantages of using the assessments in the *Modern Language Skills for Work* scheme is that the use of non-verbal strategies is incorporated into the assessment. Once the pupils master such skills as selecting key words, transferring language and using non-verbal strategies to convey their message, they begin to experience success in communicative tasks. They then gain enormously in confidence and want to have a go at some more.

> We had completed the 'Initial Contacts' module and the assessments had been successfully completed. They were very pleased with themselves.
> *We'll have a go at another of those modules - then we'll do GCSE* - deep down, that's what they wanted - to 'do' GCSE like everyone else.

Work in a variety of ways

Whole class teaching

The pupils in these classes often represent a variety of needs. We are therefore catering for a wide ability range which can be difficult in a whole class situation.

Yet there is a place for whole class teaching. Some things are more efficiently taught to the whole group at once. Some of the presentation and practice activities mentioned in chapter 6 are most effective and enjoyable as a whole class activity. However, it can be exhausting attempting to entertain and animate these pupils as a whole group, because their concentration span is very short and their capacity for disrupting, even bringing the lesson to a complete halt, is impressive!

Attendance is also a problem. Pupils who have been away come in, don't understand what's going on and this can lead to disruption of the whole class. Even if it doesn't and the teacher is up front teaching the whole class he/she cannot give individual attention to those who need it.

You could consider a mixture of whole class, group, pair and individual work and in this way give your pupils experience in different ways of working.

 ### How do we group them?

★ Self chosen groupings can be productive.
★ Friendship groups can work and offer security.
★ There is no need to break natural working partnerships which already exist.

If you want to de- and reconstruct groups, taking names or numbers from a hat can reduce the sense of teacher domination and also avoid the risk of the same pupils being rejected every time. This becomes an exercise in personal and social skills, because in encouraging them to group together and to work with different people at times, we are teaching them to be sensitive to each other's needs.

Miss, you know why people moan about working with him, don't you?
No?
Well he....
Well could you just let him in with your group for the moment, it's a shame to be left out.
O.K.

In fact, the teacher could look at the constitution of the class and at individual personalities to decide how to group them. De- and reconstructing groups does expose the pupils to different ideas and working methods.

When planning our programme of work we could earmark activities which could be carried out by pupils either individually or independently of the teacher in groups.

▶ My room isn't big enough, the desks are all jammed together - it's impossible to have them in groups.

Of course, it is much easier if the pupils can divide themselves into smaller units and find their own space. It is, however, of great benefit if a situation can be created where they are working in smaller units on the different tasks which they have selected. There are two main reasons for this:

- They respond better when able to choose their own task and their own way of working. Also, if we want each pupil to find out how he/she learns best, then we need to give individual help. We cannot do this in a class/teacher situation.

- We take the focus from ourselves and therefore diffuse possible confrontations. Even if they are jammed together in a cramped room, the focal point for the pupils becomes the small group, or the partner they are working with and the task in hand. This makes it less easy for the latecomer or the disruptive character to shout across what we are saying and even, as I said, bring the whole lesson to a halt.

> We had been working in groups all lesson, the motivation was high and most had worked very hard. I then called them all together for the last ten minutes to discuss future plans. They **would not** sit down properly - one lay full length across a table with his head and feet hanging over each end - and **no-one was listening to me!**

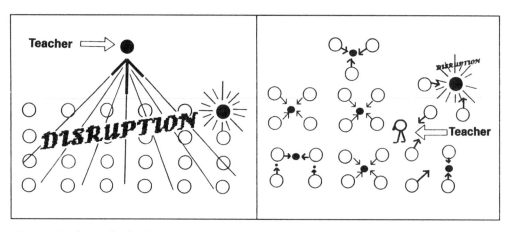

Fig. 1 - Teacher as focal point   Fig. 2 - Task as focal point

Disruption is more limited to individual groups when pupils are working independently.

▶ *How can we keep control?*

As long as the organisation and monitoring of tasks is tightly controlled then you find that, whilst the pupils are working in their own small units, the scope for disrupting the whole class is considerably lessened.

As long as the activities we have given them are meaningful and the instructions clear, then they will be so interested in what they are doing that they will ignore the other groups.

Our perception of pupil activity around the room needs to be flexible and informed. They will not any more all be sitting facing us (if they were before!), they may need to move around. They may want to sit on the floor to work. We need in these circumstances to expect and accept a variety of behaviours.

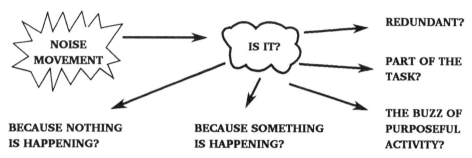

NOISE
MOVEMENT

IS IT?

REDUNDANT?

PART OF THE TASK?

BECAUSE NOTHING IS HAPPENING?

BECAUSE SOMETHING IS HAPPENING?

THE BUZZ OF PURPOSEFUL ACTIVITY?

We will need to make sure that pupils know exactly where to go for reference materials. One pupil could be responsible for resources and help the others find what they need. We need to be careful that the activities do not require instant teacher presence. If a board game is being played, for example, then one pupil has the answer sheet and judges the answers.

We need to arrange the activities so that we can decide on our own movements in the classroom, rather than being at the beck and call of everyone at the same time.

I decided they would spend a lesson working in pairs on Teach and Test cards with numbers. There were several sets. 1-20, 21-40, 41-60 and so on. The idea was that when they had tested each other on a set and got them right they were to come to me for a final check. This was chaotic. They thought they knew the numbers so couldn't be bothered to check each other properly, so when they came to me, I got involved in teaching them the numbers they didn't know and then they all wanted me at once. I had made several misjudgements here.
1. The numbers should have been in some kind of context.
2. I was asking them to go over old ground.
3. I had got myself tied up in the proceedings.

However, it was also a Monday morning first lesson after half term **and** it was the 5th November!

Sometimes things work and sometimes they don't. Sometimes there is no obvious reason. There are influences of personality, outside events. Pupils import problems from home, so sometimes small groups will break down because of disruption, but this would be worse in a whole class situation.

 ### *They don't seem to be learning much!*

In the early stages you are training the pupils to deal with their study skills and the management of resources. These are very positive cross curricular skills. Any additional learning is a bonus. It's worth again asking ourselves how much learning has taken place in the whole class situation. Individuals will often avoid speaking in the target language in front of the whole class, and respond better in a small group which offers a more supportive, less threatening environment.

 ### *How do we monitor their progress?*

As we said before, the pupils need constant feedback. This could come not only from us but also from their peers.

These group activities could appear on the progress chart as described earlier and there could be a highly visible chart in the room on display showing **activities attempted** by the groups.

Pupils could evaluate their own efforts from video recordings taken of their activity.

If the activity is a listening exercise, for example, answer sheets could be made available so the pupils could mark their own effort.

Use of the target language in the classroom

By 1995 in your school, a whole department policy on the use of the target language will have been in place for three years. The 1995 cohort will therefore be accustomed to the target language being used. But if we are teaching these groups in year 10 **now** and if they have been used to the use of English for the running of their modern language lessons, then we need to tread carefully.

Failure to understand very quickly leads to frustration which, with these pupils, can vent itself in disturbing ways at times. There are several ways in which we can aim at using more and more of the target language for lesson management.

We need to develop the situation where the pupils become receptive to using the target language for the organisation of the lesson. This depends upon the kind of working relationship we have developed.

We could gradually build up their repertoire of day to day classroom language by actively teaching it using the strategies outlined in chapter 6.

Much of our foreign language input will need to be backed up by demonstration, mime and other strategies to make it comprehensible. Often we can turn our instructions into an interpretation exercise where the pupils try to figure out what we are saying and piece it together between them.

We will need to avoid setting up complicated activities in the target language. We will need to provide effective activities with simple instructions which are easy to operate. As the pupils become familiar with the operation of an activity the instructions for it become superfluous. So, we can start with a small repertoire which we can use in different topics and contexts and gradually increase it. The larger projects could perhaps be discussed in the ten minutes designated at the end of the lessons for evaluation and general discussion.

Useful strategies and activities can be found in the CILT Pathfinders:

Yes, but will they behave? Managing the interactive classroom
Susan Halliwell.
On Target: teaching in the target language,
Susan Halliwell & Barry Jones.
Communication re-activated: teaching pupils with learning difficulties,
Bernardette Holmes.

4.   Creating appropriate activities

We need to make sure that the pupils see the language they are going to learn as **their own language** and that they see a **valid purpose** in learning it.

At the presentation stage of language ...

- let them find out for themselves what they need to learn.
- let them show us what they know already.

At the practice stage ...

- give them the opportunity to enjoy challenges and games.

  Include activities involving:
  - ★ speculation
  - ★ remembering
  - ★ timing
  - ★ guessing
  - ★ beating the teacher

- give them the opportunity to handle items or cards.

  Let them:
  - ★ manipulate language by moving pieces of card
  - ★ win cards/items from class members
  - ★ swap cards/items
  - ★ play card games
  - ★ play board games
  - ★ manipulate acetate cut-outs on the OHP

- appeal to the physical aspect:
  - ★ make language memorable through mime and rhythm
  - ★ give them the opportunity to guess mimes
  - ★ give them the opportunity to act out scenes

- include their ideas in the lesson.

  Give them opportunities to:
  - ★ take on responsibility
  - ★ use their imagination
  - ★ contribute their ideas
  - ★ create materials for real purposes

A word about using coursebooks

There are now some exciting coursebooks coming on to the market which target low attainers in years 10 and 11. You'll find material in them that you can adapt for your particular pupils, taking into account your local needs and interests.

You will also have existing coursebooks which contain a good deal of material you can use. If you take into account the criteria you set yourself in the creation of activities for these pupils and then look at the possibilities in these books, you'll see that with a slight twist you can turn an exercise into a more exciting activity.

Here are three examples:

★ Listening and reading comprehensions with questions attached

These can be turned into speculation games. The pupils read the questions and speculate on the answers before hearing or reading the passage. Then they will have a reason to do the latter and it will be more fun.

★ The listening grid

In some types of grid, the pupils could speculate where the next tick will be. This happened whilst I was teaching a class in a school for the Emotionally and Behaviourally Disturbed. After the third utterance on the tape, they spontaneously began to guess where the next tick would come, so we turned it into a guessing game.

★ Put the following into the correct order...

Exercises which involve re-ordering language, or anagrams can be copied out onto card, which can then be physically manoeuvred into the correct order. This makes the exercise both more enjoyable and more manageable.

Choosing coursebooks

The ideal situation is to have plenty of material to dip into. If, however, you are limited to the use of one coursebook perhaps the following criteria may help in selecting one.

★ It's not necessarily the 'simplest' looking textbook that is most appropriate.

★ Check, however, that the book is easy to follow and has clear, attractive pages that catch the eye of a teenager.

★ Is the content set at their maturity level?

★ Is the content relevant to their experience?

★ Look at the teachers' resource file. Is there plenty of varied material in there that you can adapt for your class? Is it packed with suggestions for teaching ideas?

★ Is the course tied in closely with the statutory requirements of the National Curriculum?

A few common problems

Before we choose our activities let's just glance at a few common problems experienced when teaching these classes.

▶ *They all drift in when they feel like it, and when I finally get them settled down, someone else arrives and we have to start all over again.*

Try on occasions starting the lesson with group work. Have a list of choices available, and as they come in entice them to get started. If you are successful, as the others arrive, you can deal with them because the rest are busy and working independently. Often the latecomers are drawn over to what's already going on feeling they have been left out. It's like the play school approach and can sometimes work quite well with these young adults!

▶ *If I give them pair work to do, they just sit and chat!*

★ It would help to make sure that the task involves more than language practice. Build in incentives.

★ If you have the space, try the form of pairwork where you divide the whole class into A and B alternately. Get all the A's to stand. The B's stay seated. A performs the dialogue to B next to him/her until you shout 'change!' then A has to move clockwise to the next B and perform the dialogue on his/her card.

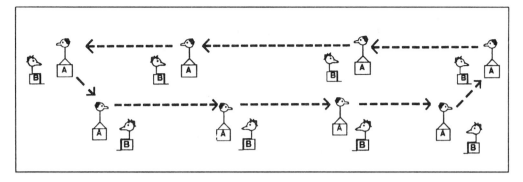

In this situation, you are in control of the movement in the room, you are encouraging them to mix with each other and they don't have time to get into conversation with their friends.

► *If we do games they just go over the top!*

There are many things we need to take into consideration when organising games:

★ Involvement

If individuals do not have enough opportunity to participate, they will get bored and disrupt the rest. Games such as 'noughts and crosses' on the board have this danger. You could arrange it so that you have groups collaborating on the moves of the game, or you could arrange it as a group game to be run independently of the teacher.

★ Concentration span

Remember, these pupils have a very short concentration span, so you need to listen and watch carefully for signs of restlessness and be prepared to change the activity.

★ Cheating!

These pupils are particularly sensitive to this and we need to be careful that our games are 'cheatproof' and can be **seen to be so**!

★ Failure

Sometimes it's not a good idea for the game element to depend on the ability to perform in the language. Rather than fail some pupils would avoid joining in the game. We need to be sensitive here. Games can be devised where the winning depends on the chance of the game although the player must use the foreign language to play it.

★ Confusion

It's a good idea to use games they already know well, especially adaptations of TV games. You don't need to explain the rules. Otherwise, keep the operation of games simple.

★ Overkill

We need to get a balance in our activities. Too much of a good thing can become boring.

★ Language

The effectiveness of a game should be judged by its linguistic value. How much language is it in fact generating?

▶ *I haven't the time to be making all these materials!*

Make sure that the materials you prepare are durable and, where possible, create several activities from the same items. For instance, a set of pelmanism cards can be used for snap, teach and test or a game of mastermind. (See Activity 12, chapter 6.)

Get the pupils to make materials. This will involve them in purposeful activities. They could make wordsearches for each other to solve and coded dialogues for each other to perform. (For coded dialogues, see Activity 14, chapter 6.).

▶ *I took ages preparing a brilliant lesson and they were dreadful - I couldn't do a thing with them!*

We need to remember that, even though we can improve the attitude of these classes by motivating them and giving them confidence in themselves, we still have to contend with what they bring with them into the lesson. They will **continue** to be moody, impulsive and generally volatile. Their behaviour will **continue** to be influenced by what has happened at home or in the yard at break. The same lesson could be a roaring success on another day. So, although we should evaluate carefully our pupils' reactions to our lessons, we must not always blame ourselves if things go wrong.

5.   Techniques for presenting language

Getting the pupils to generate the language themselves

The teacher presents the topic and the setting and, with the pupils, decides upon the objectives - or goals. That is, the teacher decides **with** the pupils what they will need to know, understand and be able to do in the situation and topic they have chosen.

The pupils work in groups or pairs and note down language they associate with it. They could write the words they know already, use dictionaries or give the words in English.

Their ideas are then pooled and form the basis of the language learning programme for that topic area.

Here are two examples.

A Spanish lesson

The topic was 'Holidays we have spent'. The class was not yet familiar with the perfect tense. The lesson went as follows:

★ The teacher and the pupils discussed the kind of things people would talk about when discussing holidays.

★ Five categories were chosen: the beach,   the accommodation, the town,
                                 the evenings,   the weather.

★ The pupils were then divided into five groups and each group took a category.

★ They noted in Spanish (dictionaries were used) or in English all the things which they would want to talk about under these categories.

★ The teacher then took contributions from each group and pooled all the ideas on the overhead projector. When the pupils gave him English words, he translated them into Spanish, and where they gave him Spanish verbs in the present tense, he converted them into the perfect, indicating that we were talking about **last year**.

★ The teacher then went through the list checking comprehension and pronunciation with the help of mime and other clues.

★ As the class copied this list into their books, accompanied by the English meaning, he wrote some of the Spanish expressions on pieces of card and put them in a hat.

★ When the pupils had finished copying down the list they played a game of charades with the words in the hat.

This was a class of low attainers who had been very difficult to motivate. Here they were working with enthusiasm. The language they were using had been chosen **by them**, it was **their** language. They were learning to use the perfect tense with expressions **they had chosen to use**.

A French lesson

This was with my own class and the topic was 'Looking after the foreign visitor in places of work in the locality.'

I asked them to note down all the kinds of things they thought they would need to be able to say if a foreign visitor were to come into their place of work. They wrote it all down in English, apart from one, who looked in his dictionary and found 'bienvenu!'. Below are examples of what they wrote. The examples are taken from several books.

Getting the pupils to audit the language they will need

This, of course, is easier if you make your setting your own locality! They could make visits to the local service industries to interview employees regarding the language they use to deal with customers and the personal and social skills the job demands.

Letting the pupils demonstrate what they know already

Here are two examples:

★ The topic is talking about daily routine. The teacher displays magazine pictures of people going about their daily routine, the pupils offer the foreign language for the pictures they can talk about, and the teacher presents the new language for the others.

★ The teacher presents the topic and the context, for example helping a visitor find his/her way around town.

The pupils are divided into groups of four or five.

The group which can produce the most words connected with that topic in ten minutes is the winner. You could say that they get two points if they have a word no-one else has.

Letting the pupils deduce meanings

The topic, again, is 'Daily routine'. The teacher puts a list of words on the overhead projector. The pupils will use their previous knowledge to deduce the meaning of the words. The teacher could do one of two things:

★ reveal the activities listed one by one and, if the pupils think that the words describe what they do in the morning, they stand. The teacher helps with meanings with mime and other clues.

★ reveal the whole list and the pupils pick out the ones they recognise. The list could be accompanied by magazine pictures displayed on the wall and the pupils pick out the relevant ones as the teacher goes through the list.

6.   Techniques for practising language

The following ideas are selected from a whole collection of techniques and activities. They are a mixture of my own or are adaptations of other well known and tested ideas. One thing they all have in common is that I have used them in lessons with pupils with learning difficulties in year 10 and they have worked.

The activities are sequenced according to the skills involved, starting with activities involving listening and responding, working through to activities which involve writing. Many, in fact, integrate the skills.

1. Chaotic listening (listen and respond)

Aim: To get the pupils to scan listening material for particular words.

Materials: Cassette.

Organisation: Class activity.

Procedure:
- The teacher has on cassette a passage or dialogue where a topic is mentioned and certain key words are repeated several times.
- The pupils are put into groups which represent each key word.
- The teacher plays the tape, and every time a group hears their word mentioned, those pupils shoot up and sit down again.
- When the topic word is mentioned the whole class has to stand and sit down again.

An example of a passage which could be used

I gave my counterpart in our link school the following words and asked her to include them several times in the passage. She wrote this passage out and recorded it on cassette.

The words: ***Passe-temps***. All to stand when they hear this.

Then, for each group: *le **shopping**, la **voile**, le **rugby**, le **squash**, la **pêche***.

Les Passe-temps en France

*Bon, alors, il y en a beaucoup! Si vous me demandez quels sont mes **passe-temps** favoris - eh bien, c'est **le shopping**! Comme je ne suis pas très bien organisée, **le shopping**, je le fais n'importe quand. Mais la plupart font leur **shopping** le vendredi ou le samedi.*

*Un de mes autres passe-temps, en famille cette fois, c'est **la voile** - oui, on fait de **la voile** mais plutôt pendant les vacances. Mon mari, lui, fait du **rugby**. Le samedi il s'entraîne et le dimanche il joue **au rugby**. Vous aimez regarder **le rugby** à la télé? Moi, non - je préfère **le shopping**. Mon mari m'accompagne pour faire **le shopping** mais uniquement dans les magasins de sports. Vous savez - ces magasins spécialisés où l'on trouve tout pour le sport, depuis la raquette de tennis, de ping-pong, de **squash** jusqu'au materiel pour **la pêche**, en passant par les ballons de football, de **rugby** etc.*

*Mon fils ne joue pas **au rugby** - il préfère **le football**. Alors, vous imaginez les samedis apres-midi devant la télé ai se succedent les matchs de **football**, de **rugby**, le **squash** c'est plus rare.*

*Quant à **la pêche** - n'en parlons pas! Cette année pendant les vacances, tout en faisant de **la voile** nous essaierons aussi d'aller à **la pêche** - vous savez, **la pêche** à la traîne que l'on peut faire à bord du bâteau?*

*Et si je vous demande à vous quels sont vos **passe-temps** vous me répondez quoi? **La pêche**? **Le rugby**? **Le shopping**? Le cinéma? La télé? La bouffe? **Le squash**? Le drague? **La voile**? Les boules?*

*On a le choix, non? En tout cas, moi, mon **passe-temps** c'est pas de vous parler des **passe-temps**. Salut!*

2. Listen and match - prediction

Aim: To recognise the spoken word and associate it with the symbol or picture.

Materials: Chart or OHP acetate containing pictures which represent the language being taught. Pictures are lettered. See example on next page.

Cassette with the relevant language. In this case the speakers on the cassette give the directions in a different order to the way they appear in the example.

Organisation: Class activity. Class in two or more teams.

Each pupil makes him/herself a set of ten pieces of paper and letters them A-J.

Procedure:
- The pupils look at set of pictures and predict the one that will be mentioned on the cassette and hold up the piece of paper with that letter on.
- The teacher then plays the cassette and those who have predicted correctly keep their paper in the air until counted.
- Each correct guess is a point for the team.

A		Allez tout droit
B		Tournez à gauche
C		Tournez à droite
D		Vouz prenez la quatrième rue à gauche
E		Vouz prenez la troisième rue à droite
F		Vouz prenez la deuxième rue à gauche
G		Vous prenez la première rue à droite
H		Vouz traversez la rue
I		Vouz montez la rue
J		Vouz descendez la rue

Aim: Pupils to recognise and remember what has been said so that they can spot what has been omitted.

Materials: Sheet of symbols with numbers:

Organisation: Class activity.

Procedure:
- The teacher reads out the FL for all the pictures on the chart in any order, but leaves one out. In the example above, the symbols represent leisure activities.
- The pupil who spots what hasn't been said, shouts it out.

4. Make a mime for the sound

Aim: The teacher, having ascertained that the pupils recognise the spoken language, now finds a way of helping them to remember the words, and to produce them with the correct pronunciation.

Materials: None.

Organisation: Class activity.

Procedure:
- The teacher makes the utterance in the foreign language for the pupils to repeat, and between them the teacher and the pupils invent mimes which represent the sound the words make. One way of helping the pupils to remember

31

how the letters of the alphabet are said is to make up mimes for each letter. Here are a few examples of the French alphabet. Four mimes were thought up by me, and the rest by the pupils.

A. Open mouth, put finger in, say **'ahh'** as though for doctor.
B. Swimming movement, (in the **bay**).
C. Make a speaking gesture with hand, **say**.
D. Opening curtains. To greet the **day**.
E. Point to a mess on the floor and say, **'eugh!'**
H. Flick (imaginary!) cigarette. Crash the **ash**.

K. Drive **car.**
L. Point to **'ell.**
Q. Play snooker - with **cue.**
R. Hold your (h)**air.**
T. Drink **thé.**
U. Constipation .... ??

5. Make a mime for the action

All as above, except that the idea is to find an action that represents the **meaning** of the word. For example: peach - wipe chin; cake - brush off crumbs.

6. Beat the teacher

Aim: To improve pronunciation.

Materials: An acetate depicting various leisure activities. See the illustration on page 31.
A stop watch.

Organisation: Class activity. Individual pupils accept teacher's challenge.

Procedure:
- Teacher reads through the list of activities and the pupils time him/her.
- Pupils then volunteer to come out to try to do it faster.
- The time for the pupil who reads fastest is written up on the board against his/her name and the others try to beat the champion.

7. Blockbusters in a group

Aim: To remember and produce utterances.

Materials: For each group:
a large board containing an empty blockbusters grid with each octagonal numbered in the top corner;

a set of cards with symbols on placed face down in each grid, so that the number of the grid can be seen;
a checklist of the symbols with the FL utterance next to them;
a set of red tags corresponding to the number of squares;
a similar set of blue tags.

Organisation: A group activity.

Procedure:
- One pupil is in charge and has the checklist hidden from view.
- The others are divided into two equal teams, A and B. Team A has blue tags and team B has red tags.
- The teams take it in turns to select a box number.
- When a team says a box number, the leader turns over the card in that box. If they can make the FL utterance for the symbol on that card, the leader replaces the card with one of their tags.
- The winning team is the first to get a line in any direction.

8. Four ways to speculate

- **Flashcard facing inwards** - Teacher, or pupil, holds picture inwards. Pupil who guesses what is on it gets the card.

- **Slow reveal** - The teacher, or pupil, reveals the contents of the picture slowly. The pupil who recognises the contents slow reveals the next picture.

- **Quick flash** - The teacher, or pupil, flashes the picture quickly, making it difficult to see. The pupil who recognises it has a go at 'flashing' the next one.

- **Slow feed** - This is done on the overhead projector with cut-outs of acetate. The cut-out contains a word or sentence. The teacher or the pupil gradually feeds on a cut-out until someone recognises what the word or sentence is. The cut-outs can also be fed on inside out, upside down, back-to-front. The pupils think of all kinds of ways to make it difficult.

9. Tennis

Aim: To produce words from memory.

Materials: A numbered grid, e.g. this grid of French expressions of time:

1 dix heures	2 ce matin	3 à quatre heures	4 à onze heures et quart
5 deux heures	6 à midi moins le quart	7 jeudi matin	8 lundi après-midi
9 à trois heures	10 vendredi après-midi	11 ce soir	12 à une heure
13 à une heure moins le quart	14 vendredi matin	15 cet après-midi	16 à cinq heures
17 lundi matin	18 à deux heures et quart	19 jeudi après-midi	20 mardi matin
21 à deux heures et demie	22 mercredi après-midi	23 mardi après-midi	24 à onze heures

Organisation: The grid is displayed on the board or the OHP. The class is divided into two teams. The teacher is the umpire.

Procedure:
- Toss for the first service.
- Someone from team A puts up hand and says the number of a box on the grid and the French in it.
- Someone from team B must give the English before five seconds is up, or team A gains the point and has the next serve.
- If team B **does** get the answer in before five seconds, then someone in their team must throw back another box number and say the French for team A to translate within five seconds or they lose a point.
- The challenges go back and forth like this and the scoring is as in a game of tennis.

10. Mastermind

Aim: To remember and say utterances at speed.

Materials: A set of cards. The set of flashcards could increase in size as the pupils increase their vocabulary.
A stop watch.

Organisation: Class activity. The teacher has the cards in the front of the room and has placed a chair for the contestant so that the class and the contestant can see the flashcards being shown.

Procedure:
- The teacher chooses a volunteer, who sits in the black chair.
- A pupil times one minute for each contestant.
- At the signal the teacher holds each card in turn for the pupil to produce the FL.
- Correctly answered cards are placed to the teacher's right, wrongly answered ones, or ones 'passed', are placed to the left.
- When a minute is up the class count with the teacher the cards the contestant got right.
- This could be a running championship over a period of time.

11. Teach and test in the form of a TV game

Aim: To remember and express language relevant to the topic.

Materials: A set of cards with the symbol on the front and the FL on the back.
A buzzer.

Organisation: To be operated in a small group.

Procedure:
- The group leader holds the set of cards.
- He/she reveals the symbols one by one.
- Any other member of the group who thinks he/she knows the FL presses the buzzer and says it.
- The group leader checks this against the back of the card and gives it to him/her if correct. If not he continues to hold it there till someone gets it right.
- The winner is the one with the most cards, when they have all been used up.

12. Pelmanism with a score

Aim: To recognise the written word.

Materials: A set of cards (for 4 utterances, say 24 cards).
Halve the cards. 12 of them have the symbols of the items on each one and are plain on the back. There are therefore three of each utterance. The other 12 have the same pictures on one side, that is, three of each utterance, but a score is added to each picture. On the other side of these cards are the utterances for those symbols in written form.

	Front	Back		Front	Back
	😊 6	Ça va bien		😊	
	😕 2	Comme-ci, comme-ça		😕	
	🙁 4	Pas très bien		🙁	
	😴 5	Je suis fatigué		😴	

<table>
<tr><td colspan="2">Front   Back</td><td colspan="2">Front   Back</td></tr>
</table>

Make three sets of cards like this, but put a different score by the pictures (between 1 and 9)

Make three sets of cards like this. No score by the picture. The back of the card is blank.

Organisation: This is a group activity. It can be played by a group of four. All the cards are placed picture downwards on the table.

Procedure: Pupils take it in turns to:
- Turn over a blank card, look at the picture.
- Then turn over one of the cards with the corresponding words.
- If he/she has matched them correctly (i.e. the pictures on both cards match) he/she keeps the pair and the next person has a go.
- If he/she has not matched them correctly they must be turned over again.
- When all the pairs have been gathered the pupils count the scores on their cards to see who has won.
- The idea of the game is, as well as to choose the correct word card for the picture turned over, to choose the one with the best score.

13. Timed matching - words and pictures

Aim: To recognise the written word.

Materials: *For a class activity:*

A set of symbols for a dialogue on a sheet of acetate on the OHP with the different parts of the dialogue on acetate, cut up and placed by the side in a muddle.

For a group activity:

Sets of the above on card in envelopes.

Organisation: *For the class activity:*

Put the class into two teams.

For the group activity:

Put the class into small groups.

Procedure: *For the class activity:*

- Put the symbols and the muddled words on the OHP, e.g.

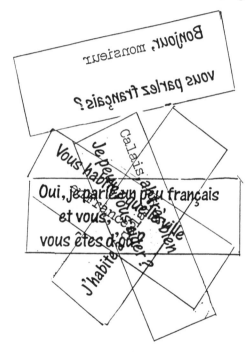

V	a	
	b	
R	c	
	d	
	e	
V	f	
R	g	
V	h	Calais
R	i	?

- Choose two pupils from team A.
- They put the words against the correct symbols whilst the rest of the class counts with the teacher.
- Two pupils then come from team B and attempt to do it faster.

For the group activity:

- Give each group an envelope with the words and symbols in.
- First group to finish are the winners.

Aim:
- To pronounce the written word correctly and speak with good intonation.
- To understand the written word and be able to use it coherently.

Materials:
- A set of symbols and words which could form a dialogue.
- One set of pictures is numbered and the other is lettered. A sheet containing the codes for the dialogues. See example, next page.

Organisation: The pupils work in pairs.

Procedure:
- The pairs decide who is A and who is B and they follow the codes to form a dialogue, which they record on tape or video.
- The pupils can then make up their own codes for other groups to use.

A	¿HACER?	Buenos días, señor, señora, señorita. ¿Qué se puede hacer aquí?
B	✓ ☺	Sí, me gusta bastante.
C	X ☹	No, no me interesa.
D	! DETAILS !	Un momento, le busco los detalles.
E	DETAILS ✓ KENDAL ☺	Aquí están. Que lo pase bien aquí en Kendal.
F		Muchas gracias. ¡Adiós!
G		¡Adiós, señor, señora, señorita!

1		Jugar al fútbol
2		Jugar al golf
3		Ir a la bolera
4		Ir al cine
5		Ir al baile
6		Ir de pesca
7		Ir al concierto
8		Ir al teatro
9		Ir al restaurante
10		Hacer equitación

DIÁLOGO		Assistant	11?
Visitor	A	Visitor	C!!!
Assistant	8?	Assistant	6?
Visitor	C!	Visitor	B✓✓
Assistant	5?	Assistant	D
Visitor	C!!	Assistant	E
Assistant	9?	Visitor	F
Visitor	C	Assistant	G

7.   A selection of topic-related tasks and projects

The previous chapter gave us a list of general presentation and practice activities. That is, a selection of activities which help the pupils to master the language they need to carry out any topic-related projects or tasks we set them.

This chapter gives examples of some topic-related tasks and projects. The topics are related to the *Preliminary Certificate in Modern Language Skills for Work* scheme.

Initial contacts with the foreign visitor and working in tourist information

Except for numbers 5, 6, and 7, these are the activities which I planned and carried out with the group of pupils who form the background to this book.

1. **Create a wall display** showing all the different countries where French is spoken.

2. **Prepare and conduct visits to local service industries** to find out the following:

   ★ The personal, social skills needed in dealing with people who come to the place of work.
   ★ The language needed for dealing with them.

   Such places could be: ★ The local police station
                              ★ Local hotels and guest houses
                              ★ The railway station
                              ★ The tourist office.

Activities connected with these visits would be:

★ Using the word processor to write letters to ask if they can visit and to write thank you letters afterwards.
★ Prepare interview questions.
★ Decide who is conducting the interviews.
★ Evaluate results and use this to decide upon the language learning programme.
★ Create information sheets in French on local events. These could be left at the Tourist Office or in hotels which receive French guests.

3. Prepare an information pack for the local tourist office

The pupils could:

★ hold a board meeting to decide the details of the contents and the presentation of the pack.
  In this meeting they would also decide on responsibilities for particular tasks, and ascertain which materials would be needed.
★ Invite the local tourist office manager to the school to discuss his/her needs with the pupils. Alternatively, they could visit the tourist office.

The information pack could include:

★ information about places of interest in the area.
★ details on how to reach places of interest by car, train or bus.
★ a map of the town with the important places marked in in French.
★ sheets of written directions, accompanied by a map, showing how to get to important places in town on foot from the tourist office.

4. Conduct a reception desk simulation using the Foreign Language Assistant, local French people, or visiting groups of students as the foreign guests. The pupils are the receptionists and fill out the hotel registration form by asking them the relevant questions.

5. Prepare a video showing the town and its attractions. This could be sent to the twin town in France, if there is one, or used in the local information office.

6. Prepare lists of useful language for local places where French tourists are likely to go. For example, a sheet showing how to explain tickets, fares, train connections, delays (wrong type of snow, rain), etc; for British Rail.

7. Help to create and write the programme for the exchange visit pupils to the school, if the school operates exchange visits.

If you would like to receive further topic-related tasks and projects (on 'Working in a bar or restaurant') and more ideas for activities, send an A4 sae to CILT Publications, 20 Bedfordbury, London WC2N 4LB.